POEMLAND

WAVE BOOKS

SEATTLE

NEW YORK

POEMLAND

CHELSEY MINNIS

PUBLISHED BY WAVE BOOKS WWW.WAVEPOETRY.COM COPYRIGHT © 2009 BY CHELSEY MINNIS ALL RIGHTS RESERVED

WAVE BOOKS TITLES ARE DISTRIBUTED TO THE TRADE BY CONSORTIUM BOOK SALES AND DISTRIBUTION PHONE: 800-

283-3572 / SAN 631-760X THIS TITLE IS AVAILABLE IN LIMITED EDITION HARDCOVER DIRECTLY FROM THE PUBLISHER

LIBRARY OF CONGRESS CATALOGING-IN-PUBLICATION DATA MINNIS, CHELSEY, 1970– POEMLAND / CHELSEY MINNIS. –

1ST ED. P. CM. ISBN 978-1-933517-41-4 (PBK. : ALK. PAPER) I. TITLE. PS3613.I654P64 2009 811'.6—DC22 2008039340

THE AUTHOR WOULD LIKE TO ACKNOWLEDGE THE EDITORS OF THE FOLLOWING MAGAZINES OR WEB SITES IN WHICH

SOME OF THESE POEMS HAVE APPEARED: COCONUT, COURT GREEN, THE NEW YINZER, PLAYNOPLAY.BLOGSPOT.COM,

SORRY FOR SNAKE. DESIGNED BY QUEMADURA PRINTED IN THE UNITED STATES OF AMERICA 9 8 7 6 5 4 3

WAVE BOOKS 018

POEMLAND

This is a cut-down chandelier...

And it is like coughing at the piano before you start playing a terrible waltz...

The past should go away but it never does...

And it is like a swimming pool at the foot of the stairs...

If you are not weak then I will start to feel like I have had enough of you...

But if you are weak...

Then this is a poem because it squeezes you...

It is a shimmer like flushing sequins down the toilet...

You can feel it rumble in your champagne...

And the trophies sliding off the shelves...

Your love coming back to you from the icebergs!...

This is like getting hit with a folding chair

And being held by your braids...

Ever since I was a little girl I have failed to rule over myself in one thing...

My wistfulness!...

It is like a suitable punishment for suffering...

Because it is better than a dreadful happiness...

Better than an exhausting chirping bird.

Poetry is like waking up drunk in a lemon yellow room...

It is a print-pattern of overblown flowers and pudendas...

It is like tearing off your bandages in your sleep...

And a good-by note left in a cash drawer...

This is when I write a poem for you...

Even though you never wanted it...

Maybe it feels good anyway...

Like fruit cocktail thrown at a mirror...

And very expensive yellow green suede...

And faltering selfishness!

When I try to write a poem it seems reasonable...

But it can never be reasonable...

It must be well pleasing...

Because it is a little unburned note!

It is like a whip brought to you on a tray...

And don't you want something?

This is a chain for you, babe...

Babe, it goes around your throat...

Now yield to me...

That little bit of love that you have...

This is when you throw your shoe at the door...

And it is like moving the old man's hand to your knee...

And it is like poking someone with their own crutch...

Your behavior does not please god but pleases your own self.

This is supposed to be an independent thought..

But it is just a strained leash..

This is a poem!

You should be able to figure it out alright...

The first theme of it is "old fashioned drinking"...

In a poem...

You have to make a charitable sentiment...

But I like it without any of that fluff...

I like it to be very obscenely old fashioned like an old fashioned stripper...

You pull a knife out of your head and threaten with it...

You sway like a child-drunk...

You take a painkiller because of the pain like mental boar tusks.

There is a conchlike muscle that keeps you from crying...

If you want to be a poem-writer then I don't know why...

It hurts like a puff sleeve dress on a child prostitute

Nothing makes it very true...

Except the promised sincerity of death!

If you die everyone tells a sad story about you!

And you must rely upon their originality...

And it is a bore if anyone will dare to admit it...

Do not die or everyone will continue to care only about themselves and not you!

I'm buying my death outfit and here it is:

White boots, tan suit, orange shirt and pink necktie.

The main thing is that I'm buried like a man.

When I die a bunch of images from the '70s will pass before my eyes...

I have to put on the right suit or I won't get the right feeling

I'll get the queasy feeling of being too poor...

But that is a triumph!

This is an extreme condition of rightness.

Like waking up in an acrobat's bed...

This is a chain between your thighs...

This is a freedom from achievement...

Writing a poem is like trying to do something, isn't it?

It's like trying to have an ungroveling feeling...

I want to sit very calmly with my bangs curled...

But my pet monster has bitten my hand!

Life makes me sad.

So sad that I walk down the street etc.

When I read poems I don't like them...

But I like them like pouf-roses...

I like them like gilt saws...

And I like them like dark brown ram shearling!...

To enchant someone meaninglessly...

Is like getting insulted and kissed by your riding instructor...

This is when your hair sticks to your lipstick and it is so cuckoo...

You close the bedroom-dividing curtain...

Gold smudges...and a gemstone powered engine!...

A great devalued thing is a plain life...

But I like it like a venus-fly-trap pried open with tweezers...

I like to live a hard life but I know I shouldn't do it...

I should live an easy life or I am a fool!

The sea-crabs try to cling onto anything.

The crab fishermen don't even want all the crab...they want money....

Even though their mustaches are covered with ice...

If you are a person you can also be someone's goat...

I can tell you all about it for free...

I can long remember a nastie thing...

If it is well done..

This is a present of tiny pretty scissors...

Which you must use to cut your beast hair...

I am a vile baby...

Look, death, I have so much delicious vulture food within my chest cavity...

I look to the left and right with my eyes and then I swing the sharp thing...

As you rise out of a cloud on a mechanized contraption...

If you open your mouth to start to complain I will fill it with whipped cream...

There is a floating sadness nearby...

Don't try to walk away from a little girl like me!

This is a recollection of flopped happiness...

And it is a fistfight in the rain under a held umbrella...

There is a way to smoke your cigarette and look out the window
but you'll never get enough of it.

If you deny yourself pleasure, then what does it do for the people around you?

Are you trying to please god with right-seeming behavior?

This is a dark dark error...

This is when you think you are earning a freedom from self-disgust through busy-work...

The poem lies on the floor until you step on it and it sticks to your shoe...

It is flimsy and soft like lemon mousse...

And semen stains on your earmuffs...

Should one everlastingly seek to appear in a sympathetic way?

Or should one avoid committing bad deeds?

This is a giggling way to throw yourself into the pre-death timespan...

Is it a sin to fail to make any money?

If someone wants to exist then they must be contented to make some tragic moves...

I did everything right but I still couldn't figure it out.

I went over by a pole and started crying...

You said I did everything wrong...

But you just said that because you were a bitch...

I shouldn't have tried so hard to make a bitch happy...?

With my poetry, I want to barricade myself from other people's poetry...

This is a chance to tell the truth...

If you only have a weak head muscle like I do...then you will understand...

But it is sad to be your own misogynist...

You continue stumbling and you will always continue stumbling...

You aren't progressing and so you have misconduct...

And you start to get excitably depressed...

It's like trying to drink a bottle of champagne in a roadside bathroom...

While holding on to a handle attached to the wall...

The swinishness of others is legendary...

But I must live under the swinishness of my own self...

There is swinishness in the future...

But I don't know about it yet.

Death will come to end swinishness...

But my swinishness will continue in my poems...!

I like to be thought better than I am...

But I hate to have the sole responsibility of judging myself rightly...

I wish that love was never extinguishable in my heart!

Then I would know I had a true heart...

This is when I am so selfish...

And exist for nothing except my own soft meat!

It is very dull like watching one's own twin sister stare into a mirror...

Success is a great dream...

But I have never been able to make myself do anything!

This is the way to handle a poem...

First you write it, then you cross it all out.

...

I should have hired someone else to write these poems...

If only I had lived during the '70s I could have smoked at work!

I am fascinated by very young children who insult their parents...

There is a strong desire to laugh...

I like it when a baby is crying...

Maybe they crying because they are so depressed...

"the magically depressed baby"

Now all the poems have their titles at the end...

You beautiful f——f---f---------!

You shake hands too nice...

So that I don't feel any moral boundaries...

And you stepped on all the cakes when you walked down the banquet table!

I like a man in a fur coat...especially a man with very little self-discipline...

I like a man with self importance and sexual grandeur...

A man who has a romantic idea for himself!...

He is just a little tramp...

This is hard work and soft work...

And I like the soft work...

And I like the hard work...

It is like being slapped with a fish...

And your bare legs going split while your head turns to the cheek...

I'm so drunk I'm seeing toy bats...

And it is like trading a typewriter for a gun...

And desiring not to be hit on the head with a shovel...

It is a dress called "the flaming rosebud"

This is the greatest of all named dresses...

This is like getting your cage pushed from room to room...

And when you cover your knee up with the skirt hem.

This is when you think you want life but you just want dynamite...

How can you feel life?

You can stare upward at god...

This is a slow dance wherein you look at each other hatefully...

And it needs to be all-glistening...

Like a gravy boat full of painkillers...

It is a very humanly amoral poem...

But this is the soft version of the thing...

This is a swirl of sequins around a groin...

But at least it is not an unwholesome paradise of charitable works...

I can see no end to the continuity of barely escaped dreadfulness...

But my head is filled with hopeful self-criticisms...

I still do not know if hardheartedness is an illusion...

It is difficult to believe in kindheartedness or hardheartedness...

I can think of somebody who has always hated me and always will!

And I wonder if there is any good reason for it!

This is the warm vanilla satin necktie...

And a white gloved hand that reaches between the legs...

This is a seeping crystal...

You have to apply a blowtorch to a lollipop...

Sometimes I get the right feeling in the afternoon...

And that's when I write a poem for you...

I like things about you...like your head...

You have such a head...

And you are not tripe...

I get the idea I should appreciate things more...

But my ego is a baby...

No more poetry...

I am no good for it...

And all, all my drinks are for nothing!

Don't let your main happiness depend upon hope...

It means your hope is buying and selling you...

Many people live under these conditions

Waiting for an emotional starlit cheque...

You have to live and not justify it any.

If anything can't be justified, you can't be justified...

You are just an ex-wonderboy...

You can try to do something...ex-wonderboy!

What can I do but pound and pound on you?

This is the phoniest feeling and yet I can't get out of it like a mirrored closet...

Do you have a desire to live your life right now or to preserve yourself?

I'm going to hug you and throw you down...on the ground...

Everyday I behave as though I am a human being...

And it hurts me to do it...

It is egotistically exhausting!

This is required to look like a poem...and to read like a poem...

But it's really just some incomprehensible money...

This is a dark caring attitude...

You can't make someone agree to all your reasonable points...

Likewise it is useless to try to be unreasonably sympathetic...

This is some loud argumentative talking that leads to no-good loneliness, unhappiness and stomachache...

Maybe my ego needs to be put on a cushion!

This is crap coming toward you on a conveyer belt...

I find my own thought process to be old fashioned but I can't substitute another person's judgments for my own.

My selfless vengeance will never be appreciated!

I'll chop your head off!

And I'll carry it around by the hair...

And you just sit there smiling and playing the piano with your prosthetic hooks...

Maybe I have overemphasized my own kindness...

Because I have a hatred like a tremblant brooch...

Even if one is selfless...it remains hard to appear selfless...

It is like painful effervescent candy...

If you are a subversive baby...

Then this is the famous disgusting thing!

Excuse me, but I am very tired so I have to lie down and fall asleep in the trash...

And it is like riding around in a clown car...

I wish I could take away your rooster-like sadness...

Yes, baby yes! I don't know anything at all...

This is so smart that I can't think of it...

I can only think of orange-colored emotional rage...

While blood trickles down my chin...

I should hit you with my bandaged hands!

This is a man with a beautiful brow...

And it makes me rock back too far in my chair and fall over...

And it makes me loosen my necktie...

It makes me cough and look embarrassed...

It is a gorgeous man with sour breath who talks too much and burns my panties in a bonfire...

Ugh, he is handsome...

This poem is a wish-killer...

It's like trying to smash the two-way window...

And trying to get broke by writing...

This is like telling someone wearing a gorilla suit you don't really love them...

A poem is all that's left of my lost loneliness...

It is like a window that looks into a swimming pool...

Or an a empty gun indentation in velvet...

And a baby gazelle given as a gift...

I am good for drinks and staring into wood-grain...

This is very painful like a miniature headache...

This is a regretted regret!

This is double everything!

It is like picking up a white telephone and ordering champagne...

And a blood drop licked off an apple...

I don't see why I must be so terrifically sorry...

With this book I have made a very expensive joke...

Every day you think you have to write a poem...

And you say "s----"...and then you write one...

And you make it good...

Sometimes I try to please someone that I hate...

So that I can enjoy a range of satisfactions...

You should always be doing a service for others...

Even in poetry...

This is like someone who pawns your minks...

And it is like a squandered money-gift...

This is the magic syphilis!...

There is no need for the truth...

Like scythes that cut through prom gowns...

This is like sitting on the counter and being kissed...

And this is boring intensity...

When I want it to be high-priced violets...

Thrown in the trash...

You will find me unchanged from how you knew me...

A woman is cry-hustling a man & it is very fun.

You have to cry-hustle because it is good to cry-hustle...

And there's nothing else you can do.

Because no one will agree to any of your reasonable statements...

And they have to counter-argue...

Then you just have to break down and cry-hustle...

There is no differentiation between life and a costume party...

That's what I like in the world. I like lovey-doveyness and nothing else.

What everyone is hoping for in life!

Now that I am so happy, why do I need poetry?

Poetry is for a young girl egoist...

Even though it is fresh butterscotches...

Dipped in liquid cocaine...

I like it like the most corrupt hand-holding...

One's happiness cannot be stated...

Because it is too natural...

And it is like a creamy bruise around the eye...

And steam-grown flowers...

And it takes you several years of hustling to achieve this effect...

This is a total lack of contempt!

Attributed to poor judgment...

But it is like a naive rightness...

And it is like mini-nothingness...

After such a long time you say nothing...and your ear-ring sparkles...

This is why I am holding your black riding coat for you...

This is like thumping on your door when I shouldn't

Or sitting the bad way on the chair...

This is when you will see what you have promised yourself...

Some people know how to write but they have no taste...

Oh I have seen it many times...

Sometimes there is a prizewinning anti-sentimentality.

There is no importance to this...as there is no importance to a dead kitten...

This is a grand gesture like being bored during a peep show...

Should I have my vengeance or should god have it?

This is soft baby clumsiness...

And the balls roll loudly across the floor....

This is like crabs trying to walk to the side...

When they have no chance of getting away...

In order to have more self discipline I need to have more self discipline...

It is interesting to see whether I can ever be any better just by straining myself...

I have to get hyped up on my failure...every 3–4 years...

These are all my gold hamster cages!...

When you finally climb up on the piano your hair starts to blow
back...

And you are just so undignified...like good.

This is one of the benefits of being money-poor...

Like some bad ballroom behavior...

Oh, I walk in the red wool corset dress and carry the machete...

I have the cigarette in my mouth as I walk down the hallway...

Poetry is my fondest stunt...like standing on my hands in a dress...

There are no reasons to hang from beams!

Pretty soon, I'm going to...unstick the flies from the flypaper and let them go free...

I like people who cry in the kitchen and get wet spot on their shirts...

My head is filled with such fluffs...

I don't know how else to show I'm smart except for poetry...

And then I knock over my bottle of Château d'Yquem!...

But is the goal of life to make everything into pleasures?

I will enjoy my life as a wretch...

Because death has a worthless lesson!

You can't use this poem to comfort an old man...

This is like looking too sexy in an uncomfortable chair...

This is when you lean over the railing and your hair ribbon falls out....

It is like being slapped in the face with a stack of dollar bills...

I like it like glitter drums!

This is some booklette of poems...

This needs to cut you with virtue...

But not the virtue of excessive self discipline...

The virtue of natural-mindedness...

It is like precious plastic flowers...

And flammable minks...

And iridescent disks of sadness...

This is meat colored candy...

This is when you stand there quite calmly holding your wood-saw

This kills the prestige!...

This is a black letter in a black envelope.

And a cloth thrown over a cheval mirror

This is a fresh sheep's heart in a mirrored box...

This can be humorous like a crotch sparkle...

You have to try to be reformed like a girl's reformatory...

Because you always run into a room laughing!

No one wants any more punishments from you...

That is the wrong swindle...

The right swindle is a poem

That has a tiny mistake in it like a cracked twig...

I write a poem about springtime if I am a fool...

I write a poem about a bad springtime...

Have I written this freely?

This is a dark peep.

Do you like this?

It is like pulling off someone's clip-on bowtie and throwing it into the pool...

Don't walk out on the best revenge!

Sometimes you feel like self-murder!...

But you are never going to be dead enough!

This is sad like falling asleep on a bus...

But maybe someone will put their jacket over you while you sleep...

This poem has the standard meaning...

You have driven me too hard with your normalcies!...

This is a long boring attack.

How can you fail to pretend to be encouraging and reasonable?

Ridiculous achievements of life!

This is when I talk and talk boringly into the tape recorder but point to my vagina...

I went to catholic school because it was god's wish...

I wore my schoolgirl uniform for god's wish...

I passed out on a sticky floor and it wasn't god's wish...

God wanted me to have normal behaviors...

But I continue to see life as a joke-time

I will become enraged if I am denied even a single fancy dinner!

This is like crying while trying on different outfits...

This is like crying because you can't open a jar..

This is like crying in a ditch..

This is when you look at the dinner table and start crying..

This is crying while wearing a hat..

This is "ow, ow, ow, ow"

My distress feels like a broken vibrating bed.

I am not a good manageress of money.

Beneath all shameful suffering I am quite capricious...

I have a buoyant feeling of splendor even though everything is ordinary...

This is digging and digging through the fur coats looking for a pistol...

And it's like a bronze ruffle going down your front...

And it's like the torn off sheer nude covering...

This is what should never be pulled out of the fireplace...!

Why should I be so humble when I haven't accomplished anything?

I like to make my own self feel better...

Now, I have lost my happiness but not my love...

It is like searching in the toile pattern for a milkmaid with a shotgun...

You must have some sort of agenda to promote in poetry!

Such as self-sympathy or vengeance...

You must seduce and counterseduce...

And glow with extreme sensual grievance...

Like an undeserved sunset...

You have to see a chandelier falling on you before it turns dark...

No one can lift up the heavy lid of these poems...

This is like being sexually exhausted!

And it is like softly rolling down the hill...

This is a knife that only cuts stockings...

This is a time of true external sadness like plastic furniture coverings...

These are self-boring statements...

People are like snowglobes of egotism with snow-glitter drifting through their eyes...

I don't believe in any salesman type griefs...

How sad and sorry that you should die when I still loved you.

This is a good thing to write...

Because it is a poem for money...

I have to write a poem with an indifference...

But it is a great indifference...

If this is a love poem then it is for you...

He was a man with a quality of a baby deer...

It was a "magically hurt" look in the eyes...

He was like a tearstained person

Being gently spray misted with whiskey in a spray-bottle...

GRATEFUL ACKNOWLEDGMENT TO STEVE SCHMIDT, JOSHUA BECKMAN, JEFF CLARK, AND ALL THE STAFF AND EDITORS

AT WAVE BOOKS AND ALL THOSE WHO HAVE GIVEN THEIR SUPPORT THROUGH PUBLICATION AND INVITATIONS TO READ.

SPECIAL LOVE AND THANKS TO CHANEY KLEY, MELODIE BAKER, BRIAN EDELMAN, MARY SCHROCK, DUDLEY & LIZZIE

MORTON, TONY PIGFORD, PETE MACOMBER, LISA BAKER, STEPHANIE AND JAY PERRY, LEANNE CHEUNG, AND SUE BAKER.

ADDITIONAL THANKS TO ALL FRIENDS AND FAMILY. ALSO BYRON HILL, GREG MARGOLIS, CK1 SWEETYEAH, AND THE

STAFF OF ROBERT E. MINNIS, D.D.S.

CHELSEY MINNIS LIVES IN BOULDER, COLORADO. SHE ATTENDED THE UNIVERSITY OF COLORADO AT BOULDER. SHE ALSO ATTENDED THE IOWA WRITERS' WORKSHOP IN POETRY. HER FIRST BOOK ZIRCONIA WON THE ALBERTA PRIZE FOR WOMEN FROM FENCE BOOKS IN 2001. FENCE BOOKS PUBLISHED HER SECOND MANUSCRIPT BAD BAD IN 2007.